Waxing Lyrical
The Solo Albums

Lyrics By Chris Difford

THE CHOIR PRESS

Copyright © 2025 Chris Difford

All rights reserved. No part of this publication may be reproduced or transmitted in any form or by any means, electronic or mechanical including photocopying, recording or any information storage or retrieval system, without prior permission in writing from the publishers.

The right of Chris Difford to be identified as the author of this work has been asserted by him in accordance with the Copyright, Designs and Patents Act 1988

First published in the United Kingdom in 2025 by
The Choir Press in association with Pennard Music Publishing

ISBN 978-1-78963-568-3

Contents

Foreword	vi
I Didn't Get Where I am	**1**
Tightrope	3
For a Change	6
Cowboys Are My Weakness	8
No Show Jones	10
A World That Passed Me By	12
One Day	15
Playing With Electric Trains	17
Lamas Fayre	20
Trafalgar Square	22
Parents	24
The Last Temptation of Chris	**26**
Come On Down	28
Broken Family	30
Battersea Boys	32
On My Own I'm Never Bored	34
Julian and Sandy	36
The Other Man In My Life	38
My Mother's Handbag	40
Fat as a Fiddle	42
The Gates of Eden	44
Reverso	46
Never Coming Back	49
Good Life	51
The Party's Over	53

Cashmere If You Can — 55

1975	57
Like I Did	59
The Still & the Sparkling	61
Back in The Day	63
Sidney Street	65
Cotton Tops	68
Upgrade Me	70
Who'd Ever Want To Be	72
Passion Killer	73
Goldfish	75
Wrecked	77
Happy Once Again	79

Fancy Pants — 81

The Loneliest Boy	82
Flat	84
Salsa Verde	86
Out of My Shell	88
Breakfast Epiphany	90
Can I Tell You About My Life	92
Men In Velvet Capes	93
1975	95
God Knows	97
Vauxhall Diva	99
Pop Noodle	101
Paperweight	103
Round the Houses	105
Power of Now	107
Sobriety	109
Uncle Alan	111
Rug Rats	113
Cinderella	116

Fancy Pants	117
When Two Men Fall in Love	119
Secrets	121
Apple Pie	123
Let's Be Combe Avenue	**125**
Shades That Watch Bitches	127
Look Out	129
Ain't it Sad	131
Models	133
It's Over	135
Save Me	137
Sunday People	139
Catch a Girl's Eyes	141
Mice Will Play	143
The Funeral	146
Have You Seen The City	148
Your So Cute	150
What Happened	**152**
50 Years	154
Gambardella's	157
Our Estate	158
What Happened	160
Guitar Avenue	162
Deptford	164
Catford	167
Yellow Roses	169
My Mistakes	171
The Last Word	173
Freddie	176
Jesus	178
Plonker	180
Pink Floyd	182

Foreword

After 25 years of excavating the subconscious mind there is little left to reveal, yet there always is. That's the joy of songwriting. As a lyricist my life has been devoted to the songwriting of Squeeze, the band I formed with co-writer Glenn Tilbrook in 1973. Our partnership is incredible and our songs are a constant inspiration to me when I'm writing at my desk. My solo albums were a journey that I never thought would happen, but they did. I hope you enjoy this book of lyrics from my solo recordings down the most recent years. As I look back I feel proud and very happy to have taken all the twists and turns along the way, it's been a wonderful journey. Writing lyrics is a complete joy for me, I may not always get it right but as a school teacher once wrote in my English book, 'you get 10 out of 10 for endeavour'.

I Didn't Get Where I am

Making this album was something I had not planned, I was minding my own business staying off the road and and not writing very much. I enjoyed my new life at home away from the tour bus and stage. Francis Dunnery came along and changed all of that, he held my fat little hand and led me to the microphone, he had the patience to help me find the courage to build the stories on this album into something very special. Each song was crafted into place by Francis, his vision captured me like a sculptor captures the image of personality. The team around us included the wonderful Phil Brown who has a history that is incredible; he worked at Island Records for many years working on a Helios Desk. That desk was now in my studio at home, a great coming together. Dorie Jackson melded our voices together, she is such a beautiful singer and I will always thank her for the encouragement to stand on my own two feet as a singer. Ash Soan, a drummer I admire, kept the tenderness of rhythm in place along with bass play Matt Pegg.

My journey really began with this album, it's why I sing so much these days. I never used to, I never could I guess, I chose not to, I was a lazy sod. I like my voice and wonder where it went in darker times. The album came out and managed to get great reviews, I was thrilled and very proud. I play this album in the car where I can hear the far cry of my childhood, the early years. Francis nailed me to the mast, there was no getting away with it and I was promoted by the future. When the album was first released I went out on tour with Elvis Costello. I was backward coming forward, but I stuck with it and thanks again to Francis I did the best I could singing sharp and then flat but singing with my own voice. So long ago it seems. I can swim in this album now, from the deepness of the pool to the shallow end without fear of being who I am.

Tightrope

She walked with the push chair
Up to the swings
He sat there waiting
Flapping his wings
Like she'd kept him waiting
As fumes filled the air
The kids in the sand pit
Kicked sand everywhere
He threw down his dog end
And he turned to the wind
They kept at a distance
She didn't see him
They barked at each other
The playing began
She bit on her lip
And he held out his hand

There's a tightrope between us
And it hangs in the air
There's a tightrope between us
We're still attached to the knots in the twine
There's a tension between us

She walked with the pushchair
Way down through the trees
He walked just behind them
As if on his knees
To make up and salvage
The rest of their lives
He promised to change things without compromise
There's a tightrope between us
And it hangs in the air

There's a tightrope between us
We're still attached to the knots in the twine
There's a tension between us
And I almost believed him
And I almost gave in
But with her intuition
She came back she came back once again
And he was left thinking
At the foot of the stairs

How did we end up in this way
Chasing the remains of each day
The push chair was folded
And slung in the car
We drove back together
Had we come too far
To witness the humour
To feel it inside
The love for each other
That shines in our eyes
There's a tension between us

It shines in our eyes
There's a tightrope between us
And it hangs in the air
There's a tightrope between us
We're still attached to the knots in the twine
There's a tension between us
That used to be mine

For a Change

We used to be useless we lied all the time
Entwined with each other
like two flames of the same fire
High on darkness
Engulfed in our lives
Two drunks on vacation
We couldn't get any higher
We sat with each other
Out under the stars
No space for our journey but where we going
We walked up the beech and tasted the sun its living and breathing
The things that evolved from the past had dissolved in the tears
We were weeping

We had time on our side for a change
We had time on our side for a change
We had time on our side for a change

You took all my feelings and rubbed them all out
Like chalk on a blackboard
that sums up all of our meaning
Lost in anger
In fear of our lives

Our love in remission
It couldn't get any colder
The kids were not born but the cord had been torn
In the tears we were weeping

We had time on our side
We had love in our soul
There was passion for life for a change
I was fleeced like a lamb
By the wolf from your womb
I was gone from my world for a change
We were lost in our hearts
With no reason to be
No new pressure in life for a change
Then our souls run away
And we let them escape
We could walk from ourselves for a change

CHRIS DIFFORD

Cowboys Are My Weakness

Cowboys are my weakness
I act all weak and coy
My heart has a flutter
Words start to stutter I'm
Crazy for the boy
In his Cadillac
By the diner steps
Cowboys are my weakness
They go straight to my head

Cowboys are my weakness
But I still crack the whip
I do the cleaning
They do the dreaming
They can't give me the slip
And I wear the hats
When they listen to me
Cowboys are my weakness
There's no safe place to be

Run free run wild
When my fingers nails get filled
I will tell him of his sweetness

When cowboys are my weakness
Run high run low
When you've got no place
I will tell him of his sweetness
Cowboys are my weakness
They go straight to my head

Cowboys are my weakness
But I'm the one who's strong
I do the thinking
They do the drinking
That's how they carry on
And I love to dance
And I love to love
Cowboys are my weakness
That's why life's really tough

Cowboys in the kitchen
cowboys in their chaps
Cowboys never listen
when they're in their cowboy hats
In their Cadillacs and their bull horn beds
Cowboys are my weakness they go straight to my head

No Show Jones

Was it fate that made it happen
Was it just the way it was
The day we met
My loneliness was lost, all gone
Did we fall from the same orchard
Could we write that script again
It's a simple life
In a complicated way, that I am
We were The Captain and Tennille
We were Lennon and McCartney
We were sometimes so surreal
But we never missed a party
Party of one

From the Marquee to the Garden
With a glass held both hands
It's a celebration
No one understands, but me
We were the Monkeys
We were The Captain and Tennille
We were Lennon and McCartney
We were sometimes so surreal
But we never missed a party
Party of one

I was living in the back of my mind
Rolling Stone were saying we were so sublime
I couldn't hang about and be great with
Compared to others we never got covers on tunes
We were Simon and Garfunkle
We were the Monkeys
We were The Captain and Tennille
We were Lennon and McCartney
We were sometimes so surreal
But we never missed a party
Party of one

Jumping from the tour bus
Neon everywhere
Running down the corridors
With fingers in your hair
Kiss the girls and make them cry
And leave them all hanging there

A World That Passed Me By

When the brain is saying no
But the heart is saying yes
You don't listen to your feelings
As you both stand there undressed
When gravity is pulling
At the flesh upon your bones
You take every chance your given
As you stand beneath your comb
Then you think about computers
And your favourite football team
And you hope to keep your end up
to fulfil her every dream
The moon is on your pillow
And her voice is like a song
The words sound so familiar
But you may have got them wrong
It's the love that we were born with
The love that made us cry
I can only watch in wonder
at the world that passed me by

When the cradle rocks so gently
And your friends stop coming round

You retreat into the sofa
As the late nights wear you down
Now the music in the background
As your hair is getting trimmed
On the salad and the sushi
Thinking hey you look so prim
But the quality is weakened
By the hours that you spend
Trying to build a million bridges
that you know you'll never mend
Is it fatal are you happy
Can your family take the strain
On the edge of sweet existence
With your fingers in the flame
With your feet up on the table
You can watch the seconds fly
Do you feel as if your living
in a world that passed you by

All the drugs and all the drinking
All the tours around the world
Every heart I have invaded
Every precious little pearl
When you travel all this distance
Do you ever think you've stopped
Even when your destination
Isn't where you thought you'd drop
It's a journey of a lifetime
On a jet stream of release
I'm just happy to be breathing
now my chances have increased

Chris Difford

For a day that's filled with promise
For a day that's full of soul
Where the boundaries are not broken
By a challenge or a goal
It's a spiritual journey it keeps me so alive
I'm no longer chasing shadows
in a the world that passed me by

One Day

Flying model aeroplanes
Landing on the window sill
Listening to the milkman
On the doorstep with his pint of milk
Fear was not a word I knew
Jumping from the highest tree
All of my imaginary friends who liked to jump with me
One day everything will be all right
One day…

First time that I got to fly
Mother cried into her sleeve
Liverpool as way below
Silver wings that kept us high
All my dreams were shattered there
When we flew above the sea
Never thought this world would spark the puer that's
    inside of me
One day everything will be all right
One day my world will get to meet the sky
One day

CHRIS DIFFORD

If wishes were light
Then darkness would shine all around me
If living was sweet
We'd all still be living in honey
When it all seemed so simple and free
I got attracted to the other side of me

One day
Sometime
Some place

Crying at the check in gate
Praying for serenity
Looking at the great white clouds waiting in the sky above
Thinking I might not return
If wishes were light
Then darkness would shine all around me
If living was sweet
We'd all still be living in honey
When it all seemed so simple and free
I got attracted to the other side of me
One day these wheels are going to touch the ground
Sometime I'd like to be back down on earth
Someday I'll fly that model aeroplane
One day, one day

Playing With Electric Trains

When I was crowned a mummy's boy
by friends I didn't like
I made a meal of trips to school
upon my father's bike
And I used to sit between his legs
perched on a piece of wood
And if it ever rained on us I slipped beneath his hood
At home the radio was on
it wall papered all those years
the world was such a simple place with music to my ears

From Julie Andrews to Jerry Garcia life was all fun and
games I was out of my head, and underneath my bed
playing with electric trains

I met my friends at Sunday school
and playing on the field
inside my bedroom there I found
the future was concealed
My records stacked up in a pile
collected from the chart
With pictures pinned up on the wall
I found my beating heart

And at home the stereo was on
my feet stomped the floor
A Fender willow cricket bat had left me wanting more

Kneeling with my torch light turning my transformer
Sleeping with my wet dreams
with my eyeballs stuck in readers' wives
Pubic hairs were proudly counted every day I woke
Manhood took me slowly down and down and down

I chased the girls and made them
cry my hair grew down my back
The contents of my teenage years
were spent down in the sack
And I played guitar and formed a band
I puked up all night long
As people came to sit and stare
while I raced through my song
At home there was sadly nothing on
my childhood had to end
The Sound of Music passed me by
just like the Grateful Dead

From Julie Andrews to Jerry Garcia life was all fun and games I was out of my head, and underneath my bed playing with electric trains

Climbing in that photograph I can touch my stupid face
I chose the road to here and now
and this very special place
Where all I am is all I breathe
it's a sober world I chase
So I can fix these broken tracks
playing with electric trains

Lamas Fayre

We caught the ferry from Stranraer to Larne
Over the great waves out under the stars
To sleep in a cabin and look for the shore
At six in the morning when I was a boy
Mother would lead me and take me in her hand
Combing my parting while back on dry land
We caught the showers that fell on the beach
Sunshine we dreamt of was so out of reach
On Irish mountains the coaches would climb
We'd write out postcards as the drivers unwind
And mother was drinking with her friends at the bar
And I'd run them around but I wouldn't go far

We caught the Ocean that flew on the wind
We sat together and we let the day in
She prayed in her silence for all who she knew
This beautiful landscape was all for my view
And mother would take me to see Lamas Fair
Gypsies would see me and they'd play with my hair
I heard my fortune told so simply there

The rain was falling on the heather and gorse
I had my ice cream with the chocolate sauce
Father was frowning a bag on his back

The happier he got the more that he drank
Fiddles were playing in the opposite bar
I had my crisps and lemonade in the car
Down to the causeway where giants once roamed,
I'd chase the crabs just before they got stoned
My father my mother my brothers and me
So young and simple in my memory

Trafalgar Square

Time is racing right along
Like clouds that pass above
We never stop to touch the sky
Life can blow us like the wind
We're smiling on a swing
Then crying on the ground below
Every time that we fight
I bite on my tongue
Every time that we scream and shout
I'm the clown who's wrong
But when this is all over I'll meet you in Trafalgar Square

Love is something we expect
To live inside our heads
As well is in our tender hearts
Hope will never ever drift
We'll learn to own the gift
With pictures of our children's lives
Every time that you sleep
I'll be by your side
Every time that we wave good bye
I'm the guy who's gone from your life but not for long
Stop the world and let's get off let's try to understand

We have to live with ourselves
Every time that you cry
I'll try to be there
Every time that we laugh out loud
I come round to our love once again
And when this is all over
I'll meet you in Trafalgar Square

Parents

They danced together
On vinyl and on stone
That secret moment
That held them both together
That was their life exciting without vogue
Dancing like babies on two elastic bands in the night
Oh how they danced
Oh how they cried
They got so many dreams

The record player
Span underneath the lampshade
The Mantovani
Trickled through the amp
Those velvet shoulders
Glided in thin air
Smoking Bachelors drinking from the bottles on the shelf

Oh how they danced
Oh how they cried
They got so many dreams
Oh how they sent me to bed
Oh how they played with my games
They got so many dreams

They flew away like paper in the wind
Life is too short to mess around with anything in love
Oh how they danced
Oh how they cried
They got so many dreams
Silence is ours
Each image that fades
Returns like a moon
My children look on
As I'm looking back
They see in my eyes
Oh how he dances
Oh he cries
He's got so many dreams in his eyes

The Last Temptation of Chris

Boo Hewerdine is such a great person to work with, he sits by my side I type the words he strums and he sings. It's like having a suit made. He cuts the cloth and within a few weeks I'm mincing about in the songs we have crafted, written side by side over a cup of mint tea and toast. He gets me, not that easy I'm sure. I remember being in Brighton and meeting Boo from the station, we would sit at my desk and write and then eat and then write more, and then we would find a studio and cut the tracks with our mates; what a great idea, a thrill indeed. John Wood who recorded Squeeze back in the day and Nick Drake further back in the day came down from Scotland to twist the knobs and record the songs, it was such a pleasure working with him, but sadly he got caught up with Pro tools and the massive handbook it came with; it was like watching a postman try and deliver a baby through a letter box. I loved his work on this album and all who sailed in her; Tim Wellar on drums, a big thrill for me to work with Tim, he was thoughtful and focused. Boo did most of the playing and laid down the guides for me to sing. Hard work indeed.

Eastbourne was our home while we recorded and the nice sandwiches from next door. I had brass on a few tracks, I was on fire. Who would have thought. Boo and I toured and once again Dorie came along to hold my voice in hers, how lovely for me and how lucky. She is such an angel, the vocal headmistress. We toured around the country with our songs all wrapped up in the small rooms with tiny PA's. It was where we were supposed to have been. Stiff Records put the album out and today it gets played alongside its predecessor in the car. Boo and I have a suit, we wear it well, I sometimes wear it in my every day, when I stand alone on the stage I try to lean on the shadows of my great friends who helped me get where I am, with all the temptations that fall at my feet. I'm a lucky bugger when all said and done and this album speaks of honesty and friendship.

Come On Down

She said she saw the problem and wanted so to help
I told her I was useless I'd tightened up my belt
She lent me so much money I could have bought a yacht
But now I'm in the dog house I went and spent the lot
She said it's not a problem I'll take complete control
We dug ourselves together into a deeper hole
And now I have discovered it's causing us to fight
I can't pay back the money but I love her every night

She said I think it's over unless you clear the debt
I'm walking round in pieces a gun put to my head
Her help has turned to anger and anger turns to pain
I owe her so much money I won't do that again
She said you know I'm leaving
I somehow knew she would
We both looked at the problem
it wasn't looking good
But when the cards are shuffled
it seems she cut the pack
With all the Kings in her hand and mine a pile of blanks

I said I know the problem I've seen it many times
You think you have it sorted
but then you cross those lines

That blur the very image you're trying to preserve
She says she saw the problem
and now she's feeling hurt
Come on down because the price is right
Come on down I will pay you back in time
Until I do will you let me stay in love with you?

Broken Family

I wish I'd been a better dad
instead of being distant
I read them books and went to work
and tried so hard to listen
But then I went away I witnessed faces full of tears
It seemed like every day
the warning shots fell on deaf ears

I wished I'd been there all the time
to see the children growing
I had to leave to save them
from the pain I wasn't showing
But then it seemed so wrong
I could have been a different man
But one day it had all just gone
it didn't go to plan
I'm sorry I was not there
Me and your mother we will always care
What we have means so much to me
The strongest love in our broken family

I wish I'd been a better dad
and now I'm left feeling worried
We walked to school I played guitar
each moment seemed so hurried

We learnt to love ourselves
we loved the things that we have done
My heart is overwhelmed
by the things that make us one

I'm sorry I was not there
Me and your mother we will always care
What we have means so much to me
The strongest love in our broken family
And who's been sleeping in my bed
Who's been ringing on my bell
Who's been running up those stairs
We learnt to love ourselves
we loved the things that we have done
My heart is overwhelmed
by the things that make us one
The strongest love in our broken family

Battersea Boys

Our parents would treat us with carrots and sticks
Just two alcoholics up to their old tricks
Mum played piano and loved Gracie Fields
She would have been famous
but we dragged at her heels
Our dad was a big man unshaven and strong
He loved to hear Gracie as she sang her song
The pub on a Sunday was where she would sing
And we'd play outside 'til the last bell would ring
My brother was gifted he had a great voice
Not like the other young Battersea Boys

He knew every opera and sang in the street
And with Sally's Army he'd play tambourine
My dad couldn't take it he called him a ppf
For singing Puccini so misunderstood
When he was just fourteen my brother was sent
To the Salvation Army to live with his friends
My mum hit the bottle as her son left home
She stood in our kitchen and cried all alone
My brother was gifted he had a great voice
Not like the other young Battersea Boys

He studied his music and we kept in touch
We still have that old stream of brotherly love
He sings for his supper, still wants to be
A voice on the big stage with his own CD

Our parents are long gone cold in the ground
I served time in prison but they weren't around
I love my sweet brother his voice makes me cry
We sing for forgiveness as time passes us by
My brother was gifted he had a great voice
Not like the other young Battersea Boys
My brother was gifted he had a great voice
Not like the other young Battersea Boys

On My Own I'm Never Bored

On my own I know I'm safe
I have no need to misbehave
And deep within I have a faith
That keeps me tuning in
Each frequency will zing
Just like a chord
On my own I'm never bored

Here I sit alone at night
Punching shadows in the light
Half a moon is burning bright
Down by the sea
Its face looks right at me
Just like a prawn
On my own I'm never bored

I hear the drunk and see his shape
He never stops to take a break
He likes the brew on his cornflake
That sounds ok to me
But I must let it be
Or be ignored
On my own I'm never bored

On my own I can touch the sky
On my own I can climb a tree
I can reach the fruit from within me
Before it falls
Without getting bored
Bored with you
Being stuck with me

She lies in bed the land of nod
I know she dreams of being God
But her fingers are made of cod
And not of magic strokes
She sleeps with other blokes
I am assured
On my own I'm never bored

There was a time when I'd get pissed
But now I see a therapist
He helps me through the old red mist
He thinks I might be gay
But just like tooth decay
That feels sore

Julian and Sandy

He was the Prince of Darkness
The King of Wardour Street
His shop would run like clockwork
A well oiled boutique
He'd sit around with Patrick
And moan about Phil
They'd go out to the pictures
Cook a Chinese meal

Nattering to Fergus
Who goes to AA every night
And lay by the fire and talk about the men in their lives

He always liked to gossip
With regulars that came
To buy the latest fashions
And flit around like flames
He lounged in his pyjamas
On the sofa on his own
And smoke a small cigar
At the end of the phone
Bickering with Richard
Who never gets high
And lay by the fire and talk about the men in their lives
The cappuccino sunrise fades across the street
They'd watch the young men dressing

With his tongue between his teeth
He was the Prince of Darkness
The Queen of all the clubs
He'd mince through Covent Garden
With all the other loves
They used to think the sunshine
Shone out of his backside
He'd walk down the pavement
As the sun shone behind

From Piccadilly Circus
To the top of Portman Square
They walk so close together
and talk about the men in their lives

The Other Man In My Life

He never saw me
I never saw him
We were worlds apart
But somehow we pulled on
All of the same strings
On the same young heart
We loved the woman
Who turned the light out
As the darkness dissolved
The other man in my life
I never see how he feels
But I know how much he hurts
The other man in my life
I've never met him
Or saw his picture
Or knew his face
I felt the anger
I knew his feelings
I know the taste
We loved the woman
Who walked between us
Down an empty street
The other man in my life

I never see how he feels
But I know how much he hurts
The other man in my life
So one day we might discover
The reason why we came together
From out of nowhere to cross a line
So one day we might discover
The reason why we came together
From out of nowhere to cross a line
How could we
Have not discovered
Tripping on each other's shadows
Creeping around in the dead of night
The other man in my life
I never see how he feels
But I know how much he hurts
The other man in my life
The other man in my life

My Mother's Handbag

I used to love the smell
Of my mother's handbag
I wondered what was there inside
I once tried to sneak my hand in
To see what I could find
A packet of mints
And a picture of me
The small leather purse
And a front door key

I used to love the taste
Of my mother's dinners
Her Sunday roast was great
Silence fell upon our family
As the spuds fill our China plates
A piece of pie
And a pot of cream
Doing the dishes
Our plates so clean

And I used to play beneath the table
While all her friends would pray
I was destined for the life of Riley
Not for the tears of Johnny Ray
I was always on my own

Secretly playing my make out games
Pushing my cars along the street
Playing with the firework flames
Paul was young
And just like me
We sailed our boats
Way out to sea

And I used to play beneath the table
While all her friends would pray
I was destined for the life of Riley
Not for the tears of Johnny Ray

What a good boy, I had become
Tied to my mother's apron strings
A simple life, became highly strung
On a sofa with popped out springs
Here today, the lark ascends
Me and my life, of imaginary friends

Fat as a Fiddle

I'm never thin I'm never svelte
I always wore the bigger belt
I never thought I needed help
Choosing what to eat
Each mouthful a real treat
But when I look to see
There's a greater part of me

Now I see the men who work at the gym
They have a ripple with every limb
They never have this excess skin
To cover up their age
We're on a different page
I look like a tree
There's a greater part of me

It's so hard to put on my socks
Each morning when I wake
I see myself when I was thin
And the hearts I used to break
Now I have tits just like my mum
I'm out of breath before I run
I like to eat because it's fun
But it comes as such a price
I'm on the old brown rice

And the herbal tea
For the greater part of me
I always played the boy in goal
Cross country running became a stroll
I was the doughnut and the hole

But inside I felt great
I always licked my plate
My face full of beans
There's a greater part of me
It's so hard to put on my socks
Each morning when I wake
I see myself when I was thin
And the hearts I used to break
And it's so hard to pull in the street
But it never seems too late

The Gates of Eden

He drove his car down to a beach
And watched the people bathing
He climbed up upon an old broken wall
Where he saw the sailboats sailing
He thought the storm would never come
And he would not be leaving
Without begging on his knees
At the Gates of Eden

The sun went down the moon came up
The waves began to swallow
A light that came down from the sky
Where strangers seemed to follow
And all the lovers hand in hand
His loneliness was beaten
To put down the drink
Move away from the window
What did you think
That you would be achieving
By leaving your friends
Without really leaving
The morning came with blackened clouds
And winds from every corner
He sat alone and watched his world
Become a little smaller

From his room he saw the light
It shone down like a beacon
His hands passed like a child
Through the Gates of Eden

In his room as life was saved
He had the final reason
To put down the drink
Move away from the window
What did you thin
That you would be achieving
By leaving your friends
Without really leaving

Reverso

The boiler in the cupboard
Was making noises like it might blow
The bath was overflowing
She lay there with her toe over the hole
Drinking from a tall glass
She shrivelled in the heat
A candle slowly burned down
As she raised one of her feet
She stood up in her bath robe
Hair twisted up inside a towel
Her eyes looking droopy
Sitting on the bath tub like an owl
We talked about a baby
The commitment that would be
I'd need a slight reversal
To bring back the chance to seed
I'm living in this moment
And this moment lives with me
I went to see the doctor
To find out how long it would take
Reversing all of the good work
I had taken care of by mistake
I should have been resistant
I'd not be knackered now
Sent out into the back field

The horse without a plough
I'm living in this moment
And this moment lives with me
I turned up at the clinic
Talking to the nurses with my charm
I laid upon the big bed
The doctor disappeared with both his arms
I fell asleep then woke up
My tubes had been repaired
I crawled back to the sofa
To my angel waiting there
She went to make some breakfast
I read the papers sitting on the bed
The smell of cooking bacon
Filling up the senses in my head
The test tubes were returning
With all the right results
The pain slowly subsided
With tiny little strokes
I'm living in this moment
And this moment lives with me
The baby born this morning
Is certainly a miracle to me
Her face has left me speechless
Another twig upon the family tree
I never though the salmon
Would swim back up the stream
The house is full of nappies
And little baby screams
I'm living in this moment
And this moment lives with me
A man outside the window

Was laughing at a drunk out on the street
His bag of chips fell open
Piled up all around him at his feet
I tried to light a fire
A paint brush in my hand
The room was decorated
Like some great wonderland
I'm living in this moment
And this moment lives with me

Never Coming Back

She reeled me in just like a fish
I was hooked on every wish
I was placed upon a dish
And served up like a meal
It left me feeling trapped
She's never coming back
I was glazed and pickled raw
Drunken mostly on the floor
I was trained to give my paw
Like a begging dog
I fell apart and cracked
She's never coming back

Where she's gone I do not care
Someone else can say her hair
Is looking great in real despair
I crumbled like a cake
The whole affair just stank
She's never coming back
She must have been a nice girl once upon a time
And her father must have loved her
But I quickly discovered

Chris Difford

That she must have been a nice girl
before she lost her mind
I'm glad she's never coming back
Her underwear would always droop
She worked her way through all the group
Inside she was chicken soup
But drink made it all seem
Just like a perfect dream
She's never coming back
She must have been a nice girl once upon a time
But I quickly discovered
She looked no good in rubber
She must have been a nice girl
before she lost her mind
I'm glad she's never coming back

Good Life

It's been so long since we first met
And each day seems new
With no regrets
We live apart but that seems ok
Keeps us on our toes
At the end of the day
We have a good life you and me
It's been so long since we fell out
But that was back then
Now we have found
Laughter comes easy
As we lay awake
Then we fall asleep
At the end of the day
We have a good life you and me
We have a good life
When there is time
We have a good life
And I come alive
When I'm here with you
We looked like a couple who could only be
In some romantic play
The symbolism of the bird
Would only be revealed

CHRIS DIFFORD

At the end of the day
We only seek balance and hope
Simple in kind
With roots of oak
If love is our gift
Then there is no shame
In what we have
At the end of the day

The Party's Over

When the honeymoon ends
and the pink clouds dissolve
And the ice covers over the love and the soul
Where can we find refuge?
Where can we find escape?
When the party is over, the party is over, the party is over how much more can we take?

When the carnival ends
and the coloured lights fade
There's a sense of not knowing
if we should be disgraced
Like a wave on the ocean
we can break on the rocks
When the party is over, the party is over, the party is over and the pressure just drops

When the champagne is gone
and the curtains are closed
There is silence between us
our defences exposed
We have come such a long way
to be coiled like a spring
When the party is over, the party is over, the party is over we can bounce back again

CHRIS DIFFORD

So let the lights fade send the band home
The music plays on in my heart raise up your glass
Here's to the last play on play on

When the dancing is done
do you clear up or sleep
Where confetti has fallen
on the floor round your feet
The flowers and faces
are weltered and torn
When the party is over, the party is over, the party is
   over life just carries on
When the party is over, the party is over, the party is
   over life just carries on

Cashmere If You Can

Boo Hewerdine and I wrote some songs down in Brighton, back there again, we pushed them up and down the hill trying to make them glitter which in some ways they did. I was tempted away from the desk to write with Leo Abrahams. A clever chap with the songwriting and his production skills, we raced off with a studio booked surrounded by some great players but my head up my arse. So why did I not let Boo work on this album with me; that I don't know I think he was busy and I was distracted. The writing and the studio the cost of it all strung me up, I was out of my head on a kaleidoscope of distractions, I was not present officer, I was not guilty but yes I did murder the album, I was under the influence of hurt and pain, I caved in and went behind the curtain and hoped for the best. Thank you Leo for saving the day and trying hard to steer me in the right direction. We did some recording in Jools Holland studio, I remember the clock on the wall and wishing it to turn faster. So generous of Jools to let me use his place to record. A few of the songs embrace me, there is humour and there is some rawness, both needed to make a good record.

'Goldfish' was lovely to record with my dear friend Kathrine Williams. 'Wrecked' said so much about me and my youth, it could have said more. The song about my Dad, 'Sidney Street', was a big moment and it made my brother Lew cry. It cost a fortune to make and in doing so I never will see a shilling from it, but that's never the point. Making records is all about the art of being who you are, and this record is who I was in Cashmere clothes with Lemonade money. My manager at the time Matt Thomas did a great job of getting the songs heard, but nothing sold nothing ventured.

1975

I signed away my future
To earn myself a place
Upon neon posters
With stickers on my case
To be the one who I am
How could I survive?
Without putting pen to paper
In nineteen seventy-five

I hid between the shadows
That fell around my soul
I drank myself in circles
And dug myself a hole
So I could bury feelings
While I was getting high
Enjoying the darkest moments
Of nineteen seventy-nine

I know how hard it hit me
And how it changed my life
I threw away a family
A fortune and a wife
My confidence was lacking
I thought I had a clue
I threw up on the journey
In nineteen eighty-two

I've never had foundations
No place to plant my roots
I'm in and out of rehabs
And in the empty rooms
I fell down on the doorstep
I was still out of my mind
We partied like it was over
In nineteen ninety-nine

It sounds like I'm complaining
But I'm happy to be here
It's been a pleasant journey
That seems to disappear
With every day that passes
I'm looking back in time
And I've never been so happy
As in nineteen seventy-five

Like I Did

He's getting stoned (like I did)
He's playing games (like I did)
He lays in bed like I did, how can I complain
He's telling lies (like I did)
He likes to sigh (like I did)
Swears at his mother
so how can I complain
And the wheels turn a few degrees
Nothing's really changed
Life still looks deranged from each other's point of view
And it's funny how your kids turn into you

She's looking cool (like I did)
Cuts down her jeans (like I did)
She stays out late like I did, how can I complain
She loves her mum (like I did)
And falls in love
Loading her camera, so how can I complain
And the wheels turn a few degrees
Nothing's really changed
Life still looks deranged from each other's point of view
And it's funny how your kids turn into you

CHRIS DIFFORD

She plays guitar (like I did)
Rock and roll (like I did)
And they call me from time to time
how can I complain
And the wheels turn a few degrees
Nothing's really changed
Life still looks deranged from each other's point of view
And it's funny how your kids turn into you
Turn into you
Turn into you

The Still & the Sparkling

I love every evening
I love every morning
I'm happy to be here
Right by your side
This house is so empty
When you are not with me
Here on my journey
Where two roads divide
I love how we cradle
I love how we snuggle
The best of our feelings
Like children, just go on
The still & the sparkle
That comes from your brown eyes
pulling me closer
A feeling so warm

I love how we meet up
And sit close together
I love how we say things
That could mean so much
When I have to drive home
Why I sit and wonder
If I should have pushed you
To reach for your love

CHRIS DIFFORD

And I am so careful
To not seem complacent
To not be so stuck with that things that I do
I buy you sweet roses
I bring you my poems
I cross every mountain
To be close to you

I love being lonely
I love being single
Here in this darkness
I'm safe within time
I know you'll release me
And bring me to your heart
Where I'll wait forever
For you to be mine

And I am so careful
To not seem so eager
To not be the one who seems so pushy and cruel
The still & the sparkle
That comes from your brown eyes
Is pulling me closer
I love being lonely
I love being single
I'll buy you sweet roses
If only I'd wake up
And be next to you
If only I'd wake up
And be close to you
If only I'd wake up

Back in The Day

The day I mugged an old lady
was the day that ruined my life
I was in a big gang of skinheads
they were very good friends of mine
We were thick, thick as three planks of wood
And we did it just because we could

The night I pissed on a mattress
was a moment of disbelief
When I woke up cold in the morning
she didn't look happy with me
And I fell into bed like a stone
I wet the bed but at least I got home

Back in the day when I was young
I thought that life was just for fun
I thought I was invincible, but all that had to change
I still think I'm impossible but maybe not as strange as I
    was back in the day

The day I punched you in Harrods,
was a day that I won't forget
I was removed by a man and a woman
I was totally out of my head
And I'm sorry I acted that way, but all of it was
Back in the day

CHRIS DIFFORD

Back in the day when I was young
I thought that life was just for fun
I thought I was invincible
but all that had to change
I still think I'm impossible
but maybe not as strange as I was
Back in the day

The day I threw up in a matchbox
was bizarre beyond any doubt
I'd been on a bottle of Teachers
I was trying not to let it flow out
I was drunk but with OCD
What on earth was the matter with me?

So here I am I'm as soft as cream
And I'm still living my improbable dream
I thought I was invincible, but all that had to change
I still think I'm impossible but maybe not as strange as

Sidney Street

You went off to battle
You went off to war
At 21 years old
You walked out the door
With bags on his shoulders
And under his eyes
He hadn't been sleeping
In fear of his life
But this was the moment
When he had to leave
His girlfriend beside him
With tears on her sleeve
He slept on a blanket
In darkness and fear
His boots by his rucksack
A fag by his ear
Like hundreds of others
Across the rough sea
He feared for his future
And what that might be
But they pulled together
Like men often will
In the trenches and dugouts
On the side of the hill

So hallelujah
Hallelujah is home
They walked out together
But he travelled alone
He marched across Europe
And did what he did
Not sure what that was
He kept a tight lip
On all that had happened
While he was at war
I asked him to tell me
But I was ignored
There were no heroics
No tales of great plight
He lost many good friends
On dark scary nights
But he came home in one piece
And there on the door
My mother and brother
Well they just couldn't stop
From waving their flags
And crying with joy
My dad had come back
To meet his young boy
So hallelujah
Hallelujah is home
They walked out together
But he travelled alone
Oh hallelujah
They knew he'd come home

Oh hallelujah
You've not travelled alone
Today flags are lowered
And roses are thrown
Passing dead soldiers
As they travel home
As they travel home.

Cotton Tops

When they wheel me in to Silverville
I will dribble words I will lose my will to survive
With the cotton tops every night

I'm stuck in a room watching TV
With a cord to pull by my bed
In case I have an accident

Forced to drink soup sucking white bread
Forking around every meal
Maybe God will do a deal

Comedians come to tell you bad jokes
I sit on the sofa and grin
I don't know if it's out or it's in
Everyone sleeps for most of the day
Until you're invited to dance
And you fall into some old girl's arms

When they wheel me in to Silverville
I will dribble words I will lose my will to survive
With the cotton tops every night

Victor's just died right there in his chair
And Betty has gone for her hip and Peter's on his drip

I never thought that my time would come
Life seems to be on re-peat
As I shuffle on my feet

So what's life been for
to just be ignored?
Fuck the jigsaws all day
I want to live I don't want to fade... away

Upgrade Me

Upgrade me please
I want to be assured
That when I get to heaven
I will not be ignored
Upgrade me please
I'd like the biggest bed
With pillows everywhere
And lights around my head
With a golden gown
A seat with a great view
So I can see the kids
And all that they might do
I want to meet the one
Who made me like I am
To say his job is done
And shake him by the hand
Upgrade me please
I want to rest in state
Inside my secret world
Where others have to wait
Upgrade me please
It's all I've ever known
Don't leave me going down
Where Satan has his home
I don't want to queue
To get my evening meal

In heaven there must be
A place for time to heal
Forgive me if I've been
A stupid, hopeless lush
Upgrade me if you can
So I avoid the rush
Upgrade me please
No Easy Jet for me
And with those Concord wings
I'll swear that's where I'll be
First class, a club
Is all I'll entertain
And when my number's up
I won't need to complain
So upgrade me please
I want to be assured
That when I leave this world
I will not be ignored

CHRIS DIFFORD

Who'd Ever Want To Be

Who'd want to walks out in the wind
And feel their head being to sting
Young boys meet in empty halls
Their fathers have them by the balls
They drive them to the match each week
So they can fight and knock out teeth
It's underground like fighting dogs
Who'd ever really want to boss
Who'd ever really want to own a gun
Who'd ever want to be the one
To show it off to all the crew
So they can know to worship you
To walk around and be its friend
When it goes off it is the end
There is no place for you to run
Who'd ever want to own a gun
Who'd want to fight out in a war
Not know what you're fighting for
Your name is mentioned in the news
When you get blown out of your shoes
When you're flown home and laid to rest
They'll pin a medal to your chest
The kids won't see you anymore
Who'd want to fight and go to war

Passion Killer

We have to be quiet in the bed
beneath the duvet cover
Lost inside a silent void
when dad's sleeping with mother
Down the hall they're wide awake
You know they'll hear the bedroom shake
So you turn over and hold your shape

We sneak around in the night
and hope the kids don't hear us
When you live in a very small house
you end up with a very small penis
He's in his room with his cool mates,
They play guitar and throw some shapes
Tossing and turning under the sheets

The faces that he pulls are disgusted and demented
The unsaid fills the air, the teenager is invented
And like Frankenstein his brain is slow
But there are things you know he knows

We have to wait til he goes out
before we grunt and groan
When he skateboards into town
this house becomes our own

Grab a beer out of the fridge
I chain the door and
Flick the switch
we're off to bed with a packet of crisps
We're off to bed and we're licking our lips

The faces that he pulls are disgusted and demented
The unsaid fills the air, as the teenager is invented
The Barbie dolls that come to stay
Know they take my breath away

Goldfish

She kept it all together
she had that kind of streak
But inside she was seething
she couldn't even speak
Her blood was boiling over
with every word she read
When she picked up the message
that lay beside her bed

He got off to the doctor's
forgot to take his phone
She spread across the mattress
when it began to groan
The message shone for seconds
it could have been for days
To see the words she'd written
she'd been shat on once again

She looked into the mirror
at the fool whose face she saw
The one who gave her being
to the one who gave his paw
Like a cat up at a window
he was trained or so she thought
Put on a skirt and jacket
and out the door she walked

CHRIS DIFFORD

He came back home to see that
there in the goldfish bowl
His phone was breathing bubbles
a lonely-looking soul
A note upon the table
and the words he'd feared read:
"You can have your cake and eat it but the goldfish comes
    with me
The goldfish comes with me..."

He stared into the mirror
at the fool whose face he knew
Had been the most unfaithful
there was nothing he could do
The door swung open
then she walked into his frame
She walked out with the goldfish and was never seen
    again...
Was never seen again
Was never seen again

He's going round in circles
in circles all the time
He's breaking hearts behind
him and leaving them behind
He doesn't know the reason
he's never had a goal
And so he keeps on swimming
around the goldfish bowl
Around the goldfish bowl

Wrecked

Wrecked, wrecked
Wrecked, wrecked
I got out of bed my hair like a ham
She stood in the shower the soap in her hand
I cleaned my teeth like the good boy I am
Poured out the tea in two mugs
Still feeling the weight of the drugs

She opened the fridge a magnet fell down
She poured out the juice and walked into town
While I stayed at home in my dressing gown
And filled up the speakers with Floyd
Still feeling a bit paranoid

Looking back those were my formative days
Tubular Bells, Purple Haze
Look at me now I'm as clean as the Queen
What a wonderful journey it's been

(Wrecked, wrecked) By all possible means
(Wrecked, wrecked) By all possible means

I sat on the floor rolled up a spliff
I sucked in the smoke and felt my world lift
But all of the time I was coming adrift

CHRIS DIFFORD

Like a ship tossed up in a storm
I didn't know I'd been born

We didn't eat much so we just stayed in bed
Sometimes at the pub we'd meet up with our friends
Then all back to mine to get out of our heads
A takeaway meal on our laps
Silk shirts and paisley cravats

Looking back those were my formative days
Tubular Bells, Purple Haze
Look at me now, I'm as clean as the Queen
What a wonderful journey it's been
(Wrecked, wrecked) By all possible means
(Wrecked, wrecked) By all possible means

I got out of bed she got off the floor
We walked in the park not knowing what for
The happiest days were when we would score
Movement was rare in that flat
We just sat there That was that

Today it all seems like a far cry away
From being the bloke who lives in the day
Who sings for his supper and eats from a tray
Where is that young person gone
Please come back Let's carry on
I beg you, I beg you
I'm as bored as can be
Won't you come home and get wrecked with me

Happy Once Again

We met outside The Butcher's Arms
You took me to some funny farms
There was always time for calm
In the chaos that you drove
until it all dissolved
But that was way back then
And it's good to see you happy once again

Your face has dropped but not by much
You're still talking double-dutch
It served you well when you were rushed
Into recovery
You hid there then from me
You thought that life might end
And it's good to see you happy once again

I met myself for the first time
We shook hands and talked for hours
At the top of ivory towers on grains of sand
You took my hand and led me home
It's good to know you're not alone
You're not alone

Money seems so hard to keep
You've always dived in with both feet
But somehow you always feed
the hungry with your heart
With every single spark
That fired off the flame
And it's good to see you happy once again

I met myself for the first time
We shook hands and talked for hours
At the top of ivory towers, on grains of sand
You took my hand and led me home
It's good to know you're not alone
You're not alone

Love's a room you seem to lock
You keep it shut as if to stop
The pain you'd feel it it would rot
So you just toe the line
You hope it passes time
But that's a feeble claim
And it's good to see you happy once again
It's good to see you happy once again
Yeah, it's good to see you happy once again

Fancy Pants

As a lyricist I have always wanted to be involved in a musical, and this was originally a bunch of new songs that Boo and I had written to pass the time as we always love to do. One thing led to another and thanks to Steve Lewes who was once my publisher and Peter Bradley, he of The Buddy Holly Foundation, they both inspired us to keep on writing and make it into a musical, they could see the potential of the album. I was thrilled, and from a handful of songs we raced on to gather the crop into Fancy Pants, a story yet to be told. I do have a script but it's never going to get to the stage, I wish it would but it's sadly not a reality. I love this album and the contributions from Kathryn Williams, Andy Caine and Beth Neilson Chapman. Voices of great love. We were back in Eastbourne recording again at Echo Zoo, a studio I really loved, not just because it's close to where I live but because it does everything you expect of a studio.

My dream was to play this in Margate where the story is based, the Tom Thumb Theatre seats 25 people surely I could sell that out! It never was performed. At this point things were changing in the industry of music, people were no longer buying CDs hence a loft full of them, and most labels would not entertain my songs and this record; it proved to be the backdoor of my journey where we just about sneaked out of without anyone noticing. A great shame as the songs and the story are so great. My dream of writing a musical lives on.

The Loneliest Boy

I'm the loneliest boy in the Universe
In this great big house I have a thirst
For lovers and friends and passers by
But no one sees me as I lie
Here in my bed with a thousand threads
Expensive feathers round my head
But here am I and who would see
The loneliest boy, take a look at me
I'm the loneliest girl as the sun goes down
A table for one in my dressing gown
I've had no luck I've got no plans
The men I meet don't understand
And hopes and dreams are meant to share
I know one day he'll be sitting finery
Strumming the chords of my heart strings
Living the life of the crimson kings
I go for a walk along the prom
Just to see what's going on
With people holding each other's hands
And me I'm just here an old tin can
I'm the loneliest boy and I've always been
I live inside this romantic dream
That one day it will all come good
And you will love me like you should

I'm the loneliest boy in the whole wide world
No friends for me as flags unfurled
To greet the people as they pass
But they don't see me scratch my arse
Here on the sofa all curled up
Watching tea leaves in a cup
Perhaps one day she'll visit me
The loneliest boy, take a look and see.

Flat

Sometimes I wake up feeling flat
Then I know that is that
I sit alone and stare at walls
I hear the nothing as it calls
I watch the sun rise in the east
I hate my face I hate my teeth
So this is all I have to say
I'm feeling really flat today

I'm like a dog without a tail
I'm like a shell without a snail
I have no aims I have no goals
I'm feeling flat and full of holes
I try to smile but how it hurts
Here come the fits and now the spurts
But I won't ride upon the waves
I'm feeling really flat today

Even if Bob Dylan walked into the room
And said the two of us should write a song
I would find a reason to ignore his words
And tell him where I think they should belong

Sometimes I wake up feeling flat
The sheets are white the dog is black
I hit the fog machine and hide
I just recoil and creep inside
And I can starve myself of friends
Where they begin this one ends
I won't be coming out to play
I'm feeling really flat today

Even if Bridget Bardot walked into the room
I would hang my head down to my hips
Even if she said "I'd like to sleep with you"
I'd turn away and eat my fish and chips

Some days I manage to elude
The constant darkness and the mood
I raise my eyebrows to the sun
And join in life with everyone
And when I do I witness love
And then I'm made of finer stuff
But not right now I'm sad to say
I'm feeling really flat today

Salsa Verde

Salsa, Salsa Verde
Salsa, Salsa Verde
She was on her way to Salsa
Her taxi pulled up to the kerb
I could see her legs appearing
Followed by the rest of her
She moved towards the dance floor
I could see her passing by
It was singles night in Margate
And everyone was getting high!
I was not a natural dancer but a wobbler and a coot
I liked my Tamla Motown and I wore a tonic suit

Salsa, Salsa Verde
Salsa, Salsa Verde
A tall man with an earring
Moved towards her with a grin
He bent her over backwards
With a wrestle and a spin
I was stunned by his performance but I knew I had the edge
I fanned like John Travolta my hair up in a wedge

Salsa, Salsa Verde
Salsa, Salsa Verde
The mirror ball reflects its light
I saw him through the mist
Could this be love?
Here's the twist
She walked up to my front door
We played some music in my flat
We found some things in common
Soul 2 Soul and Shakatak
My head was in the future standing in my underpants
She looked across the table like putty in my hands

Out of My Shell

He walked on to the dance floor
and I saw him muscle by
He tried so hard to catch me
with a flicker of his eye
A tuft of hair protruding
from his open ruffled shirt
He looked like Woody Allen
he danced like Captain Kirk
His arms all wrapped around me
like the branches in a tree
I knew this man had magic
as he danced his way passed me
And I fell for him
Like a coin into a well
I fell for him
I was under his spell
I fell for him
I came out of my shell
He said some very sweet things
About the way I looked
He over did the routine
But inside I felt hooked
We swallowed up the dance floor
And I twisted like a top
I was his strictly princess

He was my stick of rock
And then he boldly took me
to the bedroom in his mind
I went there so completely
it had been the longest time
And I fell for him
Like a coin into a well
I fell for him
I was under his spell
I fell for him
I came out of my shell
His stutter was seductive
His humour so unique
Down upon the dancefloor we wilted in the heat
And I fell for him
Like a coin into a well
I fell for him
I was under his spell
I fell for him
Coming out of my shell
And I fell for him
Like a coin into a well
I came out of my shell

Breakfast Epiphany

We sat around his table
In his kitchen neatly kept
The toaster in the corner
And the kettle both were red
She said "I think I know you"
Her mind put to the test
I was once on the TV
The Old Grey Whistle Test
Our band were very famous
Then we petered out
The hits were so infrequent
We lost touch with our sound
She looked across to see me
As I fumbled with my words
The past was very fragile
So much more to learn
We sat and watched 'Manhattan'
My heart began to bleed
I saw his tears appearing
As he reached for his sleeve
I didn't want to leave him
But I had things to do

I'd see him in the evening
We'd dance a step or two
I really hit the jackpot
In the arcade of my heart
It all seemed very sudden
That's how it always starts

Can I Tell You About My Life

I miss the bright lights
And I miss the stage
I once was famous
But then with age
My world got smaller
Then I recoiled
I made my fortune
I got spoiled
Can I tell you about my life?
The one I used to know
Can I tell you about my life?
We had the big house
With all the kit
Electric fences
The bush and the brick
Can I tell you about my life?
The one I used to know
Can I tell you about my life?
The one that I don't live anymore
And how it was meant to be the reinvention of me
And can I tell you about my life?
Can I tell you about my life?
My life.

Men In Velvet Capes

Draft fawn
Villain's field
Men on horses
Leather shield
Crimson gallows
On the open Weald
Magical rainbows
Trip at heels
Stark shapes
Dangle down
Kings and queens
Share the crowns
In the castles
Where time has drowned
Giant ladybirds
Hover around
Don't be afraid
Dark gates open wide
Look who's on the other side
In this land of simple shapes
We are the men in velvet capes

CHRIS DIFFORD

Cold steel
Ice and mud
Apple wine
A wicker jug
Was it freedom?
Or was it love
Or just a bitter
Purple drug

1975

I signed away my future
To earn myself a place
Upon neon posters
With stickers on my case
To be the one who I am
How could I survive?
Without putting pen to paper
In 1975

I hid between the shadows
That fell around my soul
I drank myself in circles
And dug myself a hole
So I could bury feelings
While I was getting high
Enjoying the darkest moments
Of 1979

I know how hard it hit me
And how it changed my life
I threw away a family
A fortune and a wife
My confidence was lacking
I thought I had a clue
I threw up on the journey
In 1982

I've never had foundations
No place to plant my roots
I'm in and out of rehabs
And in the empty rooms
I fell down on the doorstep
I was still out of my mind
We partied like it was over
In 1999

It sounds like I'm complaining
But I'm happy to be here
It's been a pleasant journey
That seems to disappear
With every day that passes
I look back there in time
And I've never been so happy
As in 1975

God Knows

God knows he loves me
His oranges juiced
He cooks me my breakfast
As I read the news
I'm so impressed
Two perfect eggs
God knows he loves me
God knows he gets me
More than you know
He tickles my fancy
And boy does it show
Inside I feel
He greases my wheel
God knows he loves me
He held me like a buttercup
That a child would hold and press
He touched me very gently
And I must confess
It's hard to say no
I had to let go
God knows he loves me
God knows he's gentle
His shirts neatly hung
He runs the bath water

CHRIS DIFFORD

Until I am sprung
Into a white towel
His eyes like an owl
God knows he loves me
He held me like a buttercup
That a child would hold and press
He touched me very gently
And I must confess
It's hard to say no
I had to let go
God knows he loves me

Vauxhall Diva

He was everywhere
Like a bad smell
He was the one coin
In the wishing well
Who you could never wish away
He was a flapping fish
Who never got away
But he was fast with his licks
With his balls between two bricks
He was a dreamer
And a schemer
A make believer
A tapestry weaver
The Vauxhall Diva
You should have seen her
You wouldn't believe her
He would never leave her
The Vauxhall Diva
He demanded things
In the dressing room fridge
He would sing out of tune
And mess up the bridge
He had a hat with a bell on
He had a fancy name
But he was really called Kevin
He was hippy, Biba and sheik

He had a ten pound note up his beak
He was a dreamer
And a schemer
A make believer
A tapestry weaver
The Vauxhall Diva
You should have seen her
You wouldn't believe her
He would never leave her
The Vauxhall Diva
He stood on stage
Like the queen of all tarts
His one party trick
Was to light his own farts
He left the band
For Yoga and Zen
Now he's back in the frame
With his dodgy girlfriend
He was a dreamer
And a schemer a make believer
A tapestry weaver the Vauxhall Diva
You should have seen her
You wouldn't believe her
He would never leave her the Vauxhall Diva

Pop Noodle

I crossed the Rubicon from prog to pop
I felt the stack heels and the pressure drop
I lost the groupies and patchouli oil
Unplugged my organ from this mortal coil
And my hair fell on the barber's floor
The double denim in the bottom drawer
I lost the hair of the poodle
And dabbled in a little pop noodle

Pop, pop, pop noodle
Pop, pop, pop noodle
Pop, pop, pop noodle

I hid the LPs from Crimson and Yes
I was the punk with the hairs on my chest
I was confused and could swing each way
From David Essex to David Van Day
And the girls I had would worship me
They thought I sang in a sacred key
I was bluffing if I was truthful
Until I boiled up a little pop noodle

Pop, pop, pop noodle
Pop, pop, pop noodle
Pop, pop, pop noodle

My Niagaras got to breathe again
I hung up my bell bottom jeans
Danced on the stage like a petulant child
As I banged on my green tambourine
And the girls I had would worship me
They thought I sang in a sacred key
I was bluffing if I was truthful
Until I boiled up a little pop noodle

Paperweight

I looked into a paperweight
And what I saw inside
Were all these people playing songs
Guitars all amplified
And boys on crystal bicycles
And Girls on treacle swings
People tripping on the words
That everybody sings
I looked into a paper weight
And there I saw a clown
With tears upon his little face
His make-up rolling down
I saw him singing from a wound
With peanut butter blood
I managed him with tenderness
And cashmere gloves
I took him all the way
Through all the ups and downs
I took him all the way
Kept him from the milling crowds
I signed his life away
I wasn't Brian Epstein
Nor was I Peter Grant
I flirted with the fame
Turned up on each red carpet

And took all his awards
Every after party we could not afford
I looked into a paperweight
Where tiny violins
Were playing in an orchestra
With me there in the wings
And on the mountain I could see
His name up there in lights
And so we left the band behind
And reached for dizzy heights
I took him all the way

Through all the ups and downs
I took him all the way
Kept him from the milling crowds
I signed his life away
Paperweight
Paperweight

Round the Houses

I once played the Albert Hall
And nervously performed
Now I'm in somebody's house
On sofas that are worn
A pile of boots out in the hall
And drinks served on a tray
While I play very gingerly
The hits of yesterday

In the bedroom nylon sheets
A few books and a bear
My rider of sweet orange juice
And bits of Camembert
I can hear them milling round
As I tune up to play
I once sang in New York clubs
But that's not me today

In this house
There is no stage
And in this house
They're all amazed
To see how far I've fallen
In this house

CHRIS DIFFORD

I once played the biggest gigs
My agent could provide
Trucks of lighting and PA
Would hang about outside
Tonight I'm by the angle poise
With no mic and no leads
Tomorrow I'll be on my way
To number 53

In this house
There is no stage
And in this house
They're all amazed
To see how far I've fallen
In this house

A brown envelope is filled with cash
As I head out of the door
Once there was a limousine
But now there isn't anymore
But in this house
There is no stage
And in this house
They're all amazed Just to see how far I've fallen
In this house In this house

Power of Now

I've sabotaged ambitions
I've pissed on my parades
I've never known my feelings
More than the traps they've laid
And I have been seduced by
The sword of many words
That cut me like a thin slice
Of a very tender bird
And my love has known no feeling
No closeness or no trust
I blew all the moments
That were meant for us
And God willing whatever it will be
But rejected chances
That always passed by me
And the power of now
Is not living just then
Or maybe tomorrow
Or remembering when
But to scoop up the seconds
Like snow from the ground
And smile with good fortune
That you're still around
So now I'm looking backwards
No I can look ahead
To see the whys and wherefores

CHRIS DIFFORD

The weaving and the thread
So I can see the story upon my tapestry
Where I have laid my life down
So you can be with me
And the power of now
Is not living just then
Or maybe tomorrow
Or remembering when
But to scoop up the seconds
Like snow from the ground
And smile with good fortune
That you're still around
And the power of now
Is not living just then
Or maybe tomorrow
Or remembering when
But to scoop up the seconds
Like snow from the ground
And smile with good fortune
That you're still around
Oh the power of now
The power of now
The power of now

Sobriety

I first found my sobriety
A challenge a curse
I lay upon a rubber sheet
And looked up at the nurse
The room began to spin around
And then I fell asleep
My life was all about to change
While I was digging deep

Sobriety
Sobriety

I sobered up and saved myself
From darkness and retreat
Each day was like a chapter
In a book I'd learnt to read
I hung on like a blackbird
To a very fragile tree
As the wind of change
It whipped around and so it lifted me

Sobriety
Sobriety

What you hear here
What you see here
Let it stay here
I want to be here
In my new found
In my rent free
Sobriety
What you hear here
What you see here
Let it stay here
I want to be here
In my new found
In my rent free
Sobriety
I walked the talk
And did the things
Suggested in the rooms
Eventually I found myself
Back up with the balloons
I did the best that I could do
From ever getting high
By always living in the day
Just one day at a time

Sobriety
Sobriety

Uncle Alan

What a nightmare
What a life
I had it all
And in my mind
I had a vision
I had a dream
That maybe one day
I would be Queen Uncle Alan
I'm a trooper
A simple bloke
I'm writing songs
But mostly folk
I have the stories
I have the beard
My friend's musicians
Still like a beer
Uncle Alan
He plays guitar
Upon his lonely sofa
He writes some words
About a troubled smoker
Sometimes he thinks he just might fade away
And now he lives above
The local Tesco

CHRIS DIFFORD

So very far from San Francisco
Where he tripped his life away
But that was yesterday
What an angel
What a girl
She keeps me sane
When in a whirl
She keeps me dreaming
But oh I try
To complicate things
And then I cry for Uncle Alan
Uncle Alan

Rug Rats

In the flat
He chanced his arm
The subtle lighting
And the charm
A bowl of peanuts
On the side
Steely Dan he played all night

The lofty things he said
Went like Vodka to my head

In the flat
Magazines
He only reads them
In his own dreams
Stolen looks
To see my breasts
A chocolate box
There in his nest

The sheepskin fluffy rug
His grave was almost dug

We were rug rats
By the time the candle died
We were kittens
With the love light in our eyes
We were hopelessly pressing pause
So we could see the scores
And we'd won
We were rug rats in love

In the room
The light was dimmed
As I lay there
Next to him
The hum of traffic
Passed us by
Pretzel logic
Rolled back time

The romance button ticked
Put a match against the wick

We were rug rats
By the time the candle died
We were kittens
With the love light in our eyes
We were hopelessly pressing pause
So we could see the scores
And we'd won
We were rug rats in love

We were rug rats
By the time the candle died
We were kittens
With the love light in our eyes
We were hopelessly pressing pause
So we could see the scores
And we'd won
We were rug rats in love

Cinderella

Oh what a wonderful surprise
Mascara round my eyes
Clever Cinderella
Oh but my family never knew
No they never had a clue
Not ever Cinderella
I loved the wigs and I know all the tricks
Raise a brow or two
We like a laugh
Standing like a giraffe
In a high heel shoe
Out on the streets with my chums
Oh what a perfect alibi
I can watch the world float by
Forever Cinderella
I loved the wigs and I know all the tricks
Raise a brow or two
We like a laugh
Standing like a giraffe
In a high heeled shoe
Out on the streets with my chums
Oh but you can't help feeling down
As your hearts get dragged around
Forever Cinderella

Fancy Pants

Hello fancy pants
You walk bipolar bear
Hello fancy pants
Blue jeans on a chair
Dresses in the wardrobe
Wigs upon your hair
Hello fancy pants
In your silver underwear
Hello fancy pants
A plum in every cheek
Hello fancy pants
Your clothes all in a heap
Guitars beside the hoover
Two puppies by your feet
Hello fancy pants
Is it you that keep things sweet
Fancy pants oh, fancy pants
You came, you saw, you conquered
Fancy pants it's good to have you back
With all the joy and laughter
There's love upon the wing
Hello fancy pants
Your joy bells seem to ring
Fancy pants, oh fancy pants
You came, you saw, you, conquered

CHRIS DIFFORD

You fell, in love, you wondered
Fancy pants it's good to have you back
Hey there fancy pants
Clap your hands and sing
Hello fancy pants
Watch your handbags swing
Dresses in the wardrobe
Wigs upon your hair
Hello fancy pants
Is it me you see out there?
Me you see out there

When Two Men Fall in Love

When two men fall in love
And take the vow to marry
The angels spread their wings
And up above they carry
The simple weight of love
It floats down like a feather
Their heartbeat joins forever
When two men fall in love

When two men fall in love
They are each other's feelings
With peace inside two hearts
Their words are interweaving
So they can speak as one
Then all can hear their wisdom
It's so hard not to listen
When two men fall in love

Loving life and giving back
With family by their side
To share the love and celebrate
It's such a happy time

CHRIS DIFFORD

When two men fall in love
Stars fall down from above
To light them on their way
On this wedding day
When two men fall in love
Commitment is provided
By love and happy home
That makes two men united
Their union is complete
With a ring that says so much
About these two great friends
When two men fall in love

Loving life and giving back
With family by their side
To share the love and celebrate
It's such a happy time
When two men fall in love
Stars fall down from above
To light them on their way
On this wedding day

When two men fall in love
When two men fall in love
When two men fall in love

Secrets

Secrets are delicious
We've all got them to hide
Keep them from each other
But they will leak in time
We know the damage
That they can do
The secrets that we keep
will one day backfire on you

Secrets are suspended
Like bulbs upon a flex
Like the darkest corners
Right inside our heads
We fend off any worries
Till we screw things up
The secrets we are keeping
Are running out of luck

Secrets are expensive
Like jewels upon a crown
But can we bare the twinkle
When truth is lurking round
And words are just like keys

CHRIS DIFFORD

To the things that we can take
The secrets we are keeping
will let us down one day

Secrets are addictive
Like sugar on the cane
We know all those secrets
light up every flame
Secrets

Apple Pie

He was the loneliest boy
He drifted out to sea
On a plank of wood
That set his whole life free
And then he found love
And all that it contains
The silence disappeared
With all of the games
He was the a lonely old soul
With nothing much to say
Love was just a shadow
That never passed his away
And so life revealed
The secrets and the lies
He wakes up every morning
With love in his eyes
But it's not been easy
No walk in the park
I've lit up my moments
That used to be dark
With honesty
And a slip of the tongue
I'm out there for everyone
For everyone

CHRIS DIFFORD

I was the loneliest boy
But the happiest soul
A table for one
And a bacon roll
I open the door the sun said "hi"
'Cos one day soon you'll get your apple pie
One day soon you'll get your apple pie
Apple pie
Apple pie
Apple pie
Apple pie

Let's Be Combe Avenue

Bob Blatchford walked into my dressing room one evening and handed me a Tesco bag with some tapes inside; he said 'these are for you'. I was delighted to be given such a prize. Tapes of me singing in 1971 around at his house at the end of my block on Combe Avenue. I lived at number 98 him at 92. I found it hard to remember the day we rolled tape and sang these songs, but it did happen and thank you Bob for making it all work. Months later I went into a studio and found a tape machine to play them on, as I listen to this young voice and these early songs I was emotionally attached to the young man, and where it all began. I used to write the words and the music and I think I did I pretty good job of it, the ambition was certainly there and the hope that maybe one day I would be a singer in a band, that's all I ever wanted. My fanciful lyrics guided me towards the future and in these words with no deepness just a lick on the envelope of a future more focused yet fused. And so these lyrics are slightly juvenile and not my best but it shows a young man trying to be more than just a kid on the block on a council estate in South London.

My dream was to write songs and be on stage, and here I am on stage now in that dusty old dream with this book and my onward journey into age, and a possible chair in a care home where no doubt I will regale people with my stories and sing in dribbled hushed tones the songs that have delivered me to this page. These lyrics are naive and sometimes I feel shy of reading them, but there they are. I was young, warts and all.

Shades That Watch Bitches

I rang the operator
To see if she could trace her
A girl from the future
She played me at snooker
As I waited for the phone to ring with the code
I blew the table dust and then I blew my nose

Hours dragged by
The sun left the sky
And the phone never sighed
So let's go for a drive
Put on your coat cause you just might catch a cold
You know how all the young kids they all grow old

Cat man do cat man don't
Drive my car take me home
You can erect me
The film is being shown
and why you test me
I'll never know behind these shades I'm all alone

Chevrolet Stingray
Take me up the highway
On the Northern Ringway
Never knowing which way
Let's pull over here for a long cool beer
Looks so nice I've never seen the sky so clear

This girl from the future
She became a rootin' tutor
Well, I always thought I knew her
And I forgot that operator
Did you want to steer babe and don't interfere
All I want is you and that's not so queer

Cat man do cat man don't
Drive my car take me home
You can erect me
The film is being shown
and why you test me
I'll never know behind these shades I'm all alone

Look Out

He draws when he talks he balls when he shorts
He looks like a spy with a key in his eye
He springs when he walks
So what can he do his mind is a zoo
His tiptoe feet they watch me as I sleep
And he jokes with a flute

A stone-white face a long dark hair
Cold blue eyes he stands and stares
Look out boy they're gonna gun you down
Look out boy get out of my town

Speed is a bugger he's got lips like rubber
A trigger crazy dressed up a lady what was your mother
Hot-foot round corners massured saunas
Whip me again he cries to the man
your life's at the pawners
A stone-white face a long dark hair
Cold blue eyes he stands and stares
Look out boy they're gonna gun you down
Look out boy get out of my town

I'll break you in bits
and so will the kids
Lay off of the club just look what you've done
Don't give me no lip

The sexes have gone
And the feelings too strong
Go spook up the moon I hear we'll be there soon
I said go on go on
A stone-white face a long dark hair
Cold blue eyes he stands and stares
Look out boy they're gonna gun you down
Look out boy get out of my town

Ain't it Sad

No cameras no lights
No stars in my eyes no way of getting through to you
No ride in my car with a two-time tart
no way to make a dream come true
Walking up the streets with my face and no smile
just the postcard of a place I know

Ain't it sad girl ain't it sad ain't it sad It's sad
Funny little things I've thought I never had

No windows no noise no girls
For the boys, no point in sacrificing a night
No holes in my shoes no flashes of news
No way of getting into a fight
I'm riding up the streets with my hands on the wheel
Just a minute while I change my mind

Ain't it sad girl ain't it sad ain't it sad It's sad
Funny little things I've thought I never had

No afternoon calf missing English and maths
No tours round the summer coast
No movies no scripts no waiters no tips
No letters in my morning post

CHRIS DIFFORD

Sitting on the streets take a hold of my hand
Wait a minute while I make the most
Ain't it sad girl, ain't it sad Ain't it sad It's sad
Funny little things I've thought I never had

Models

Streets ahead of her time
fashion she's never lazy
Her tone could change your mind
And the fit could drive you crazy
Models used for winter clothes
and summer clothes that shine
Models used for magazines
I read them all the time If that's alright

Do do do do, do do do do, down the runway
Do do do do, do do do do, do do do do, she's so lovely

She's got my feet up higher
my eyes don't look so bad
And my dress it looks like wire
and it costs me more than land
Models used for curly hair
and hair that flows so free
Models used for underwear
well I wish that I could sleep.
that's okay with me

Do do do do, do do do do. Do do do do down the runway,
Do do do do, Do do do do, do do do, She's so lovely.

CHRIS DIFFORD

See her face on the stations
and in the daily news
There is no explanation
why she does these things for you
Models used for TV the sort that sells cigars
Models all around us looking like film stars
ha ha ha ha

Do do do do, Do do do do, do do do do down the runway.
Do do do do, Do do do do, do do do, She's so lovely so lovely

It's Over

It's over
the singer has taken his bow
all over
the lights have begun to go out
the rain is still falling it's 3 in the morning it's over
there's hardly a sound,

It's over
The lovers look tired and cold
all over
the cab drives the memories home
The grey clouds are going
the moon begins showing
It's over
don't tell me I know

I asked her if she like to dance
and let her out into my arms
she looked me in the eyes and said "hey soldier"
What do you think will happen when
this drink you've had gone to your head
and you want me when I say, it's over

It's Over
She's walked right out of sight
all over

CHRIS DIFFORD

she danced with me tonight
I know she won't see me
I don't think she needs me
It's over
There's stars in my eyes

It's over
My shadow and I on the streets
all over
I wonder if she thinks of me
the rain is stopped falling I hear someone calling
it's over

Come back to me come back to me
Come back to me come back to me

Save Me

I'm not quite sure if my life's been saved
Whether I'm an idol or a working slave
Is there hope for me yes there's hope for me

Do I have to kiss the rich man's feet
so that one day he can own my dreams in a biography
So what is wrong with me

My nightmares keep me well informed
there's gonna be a rainbow after the storm.
And I'll get to you sometime I guess until I do there can
   be no rest

Save me like an ending until the last
because I'm not strong enough to take the chance
And forever let the children sing and dance
And forever let the children sing and dance

I scratch the walls with my fingernails
Looking in the mirror my skin looks pale
Am I up with you Yes, I'm up with you
You're moving faster than a crisis
All different lives cost different prices
I know it's true so please believe in what I do

CHRIS DIFFORD

Logic is a thing that has no meaning
to me I'm just another being
Forgive me for asking all these favours
but put me on a page in the morning paper

Save me like an ending until the last
because I'm not strong enough to take a chance
And forever let the children sing and dance
And forever let the children sing and dance

Save me like a letter from a lover
Save me like a birthday till next year
Save me If and when my ship goes under
because of mine's a future I alone will fear

Save me! Like an ending until the last
And forever let the children sing and dance
And forever let the children sing and dance

Sunday People

Sunday People out walking
Sunday People always talking
Sunday People always on my street
Never smiling always hiding
Never knowing who is fighting
Sunday People always pushing me
pretty girl walks me by with her mind in her gloves
pretty girl don't you cry
you're not living till you're in love

Sunday people in watching
Sunday people always knocking
Sunday people always turn me down
Sunday heaven starts at 7
Me I'm waiting for 11
Sunday people walking in a crowd
pretty girl sunbathing in a crowded park
pretty girl I'm so crazy I'm letting you into my heart

Sunday people seeing movies
Marilyn Monroe's and Mickey Rooney's
Sunday people looking starry-eyed
Sunday people always cleaning

Sunday people have no meaning
Sunday people never asking why
Pretty girl close the door leave the day outside
Pretty girl are you sure that you'll call for me tonight

Catch a Girl's Eyes

I'm shining my shoes for I have a date how do you do
I hope I'm not late you've got a dress right to catch a
   girl's eyes

I'm choosing a tie to go with my suit that shine in your
   eye says I'm meeting
you you've got a dress right to catch a girl's eyes

That's half the fun of being in love
looking smart for number one
she's always looking nice for you
We'll look so nice together tonight
out in the dark or in the light
she always wears your favourite perfume

My suit has been pressed my shirt has been starched
I must look my best to win all her heart
You've gotta look nice to catch a girl's eyes
I'm combing my hair and watching the time
there's none to compare for she will be mine
You've gotta dress right to catch a girl's eyes

That's half the fun of being in love
Looking smart for number one
She's always looking nice for you
We'll look so nice together tonight
out in the dark or in the light
She always wears your perfect perfume

Mice Will Play

She entered stage
With no applause
No heads were turned
As she performed
Her fist were clenched
down by her side

Jokes were told
As people roared
Her song was heard
But well ignored
I lifted her
And tried to hide

Sweat was dripping
From her nose
Some old man shouted
Take off your clothes
Her smile was forced
For everyone

Expensive woman
Were pulling men
Emptying pockets
Of empty heads
I drank alone
But shared the fun

She lifted her skirt
Up in her hands
And every eye
Of every man
Sparkled light
Like hungry men

Her foot was resting
On a stool
Her movements made
The old men drool
And so she called
A few more friends

Upon the stage
She threw her blouse
Her nylons flew
Into the crowd
Her dark hair
Hung across her face

Hands reached out
Some woman shoved
She sung no more
Her songs of love
She felt abused
And lost the taste

Trixie appeared
In his evening dress
He always tried
To look his best
She looked his way
And started to sing

The Funeral

We don't mind the smell and we're used to all the rats so damp that I just can't sleep it's like heaven and hell where the whites and the blacks and the trash just stays in the street in our neighbourhood we don't care for the rich and our counsellor he's a son of a bitch

A time to stand and reach much higher he was ten and I was almost eight he called my friend the dirty liar we put our footprints upon his grave

The middle class kid walked with his nose up high he was clean with his curly hair well we cut his lip and he started to cry his blood dripped everywhere in our neighbourhood no one leads a gang we're the sort of boys you won't understand

A time to stand and reach much higher he was ten and I was almost eight he called my friend the dirty liar we put our footprints upon his grave

But we dragged him down to where the river meets the smelly drains in the wall well he made no sound as we tied his feet and he looked so sad and small In our neighbourhood when it's late late at night you think it's a cab when a baby is crying

A time to stand and reach much higher he was ten and I was almost eight he called my friend the dirty liar we put our footprints upon his grave

Have You Seen The City

You can walk the busy streets
and see the man you'd like to be
and remember his face just for an hour
You can book the highest room
In the highest standard tomb
and send yourself pretty pretty flowers
The Pilates they lean on the wall
then how's the biggest biggest smalls
the muggers tremble on the underground
The taxi drives a Catholic priest
To worship his unknown deceased
The lovers cram the bar for another round

You can sit in idle parks and think yourself into the dark
About the problems you have on your hands
You can drink the bottle dry
and throw it high into the sky
And dress up like a woman or like a man
The post boy runs for his train
He thinks it is an aeroplane
The dealer's dodging from his corner plinth
The bus queue grows I'm at the end
I watch the signs above my head
The old man shows me his heroic limp

You can love the girls you see
and put them up inside a dream
and wake up in a quiet record shop
You can sit and watch sunrise or listen to a baby cry
and read on with the latest scandal and shock
The young fans they wait for their heroes
Dylan Jagger and Shapiro
The winter brings out all the late TV nights
The unions are out to demonstrate
And Chaplain's on and I can't be late
The summer takes me to the countryside

And I tap my foot and I read a book
My age is all around me
It's time to read my mind
all the rage is here to drown me

Your So Cute

When there's nothing better doing I'll get out a book and go outside and laze in the sun I'll read the first chapter but that is enough I wanna be alone with everyone I'll pour out a sherry cause I fancy a drink I think it's so hot and I wanna go back in go back in When there's nothing better doing I'll pick up the phone and ring and see if Susie's still around there is no reply so I have to drink alone my every other upbeat comes down I pick up a pen and write a few words it's such a hot day and you're a beautiful girl beautiful girl

When there's nothing better doing I walk on uptown and try to make a pass upon the street a funny little man sat on the underground I thought he might be fancying me I get off the train the pretty girl's gone I look to the book and then her boyfriend got on he got on

When there's nothing better doing I put on a tape and dance around like Fred Astaire A one-step a two-step I try to keep awake I wanna know why you don't even care I'll kick off my shoes and watch the TV a late-night movie always puts me to sleep you're so cute

I get off the train the pretty girl's gone I looked at her book and then her boyfriend got on I kicked off my shoes and watched the TV a light night movie always puts me to sleep I pick up a pen and write a few words it's such a hot day, and you're a beautiful girl I pour out a sherry because I fancy a drink I think it's so hot and I wanna go back in

What Happened

During Lockdown I like everyone else stayed safe indoors, I went to my shed and scratched my head, what to do. I went online and played a few shows on Zoom with my dear friend Melvin Duffy, I sat around and missed the touring I had grown to love, I wrote some lyrics. This is what happened, I looked back at my years before Squeeze the years leading up to meeting Glenn, a real turning point in my life; without that meeting this page would be blank. I wanted to make friends with my past and bring it all into view and so I got writing. Boo Hewerdine was online and escorted me down many new musical avenues, mainly Combe Avenues, we must have written about 40 songs, some for an album about therapy and these from the most recent recordings of What Happened. Back to Eastbourne this time with Neil McColl at the helm, he formed a band for me and we recorded all the songs in just 10 days, the whole album. But then after it was mixed there was the sound of nothing, and nothing is louder than the sound of these songs. Jon Kelly mixed the songs at his studio in London, we first met on the Fancy Pants recordings, a true gentleman. The recordings then turned into a musical Podcast and that's where it sits today, as no record company wants to take the risk of putting it out for me. What risk?

We hope to put all of my albums up on the internet via my website and CD Baby a kind of online HMV without the racks, it's all just a click away, so click away. I love the lyrics and feel immensely proud of what I have achieved. This might be the last record I ever make on the solo forum as it costs so much to get to hear the sound of beautiful silence. I would rather spend the money on sitting still at home, although it does give me a story to tell on tour and that's where it all sits for me, out on tour telling stories without the CD package, without the stock on the merch stand, without the stock in the loft, just a few strums and a drive up the M23. Keep coming back.

50 Years

When the fighting got too tough
I made my retreat
Back up to my bedroom
To stare at my feet
And think about playing
The songs that I knew
Might keep me from danger
And help me meet you

I bumped into Barry
He played the guitar
He had a few sad songs
His fingers would bar
We dropped out together
And I grew my hair
The joints we were smoking
Were rolled with great care

At the festival site
In 71
I was tripping to Hawkwind
And freaked out to Gong
My head was a foundry
Of wheels being turned
I was in at the deep end

And never returned
Who knew
Who cared
Who heard
Me there
That day
I found
My voice
that sound
I'd never heard before
When 50 years came knocking at my door

An ad in a window
Determined my fate
The start of this journey
That always has shaped
The arc of my being
And all that I am
Stems out of that meeting
To where I now stand

I'm grateful for taking
The twists and the turns
The skinhead the hippie
Each moment confirms
The pride and the passion
Its core of belief
I made my transition
Back home in Blackheath

Who knew
Who cared
Who heard
Me there
That day
I found
My voice
that sound
I'd never heard before
When 50 years came knocking at my door
Came knocking at my door

Gambardella's

We used to play under washing lines
Kicking leather balls against a garage wall
wearing brogues and blue tonic suits
I was the most unlike lad

We danced to Motown in our council flats
Cider and pills up the wooded hills
two party seven's a stack of 45's
I was the most unlike lad

I used to sit and read the NME
Gambardella's on a Thursday night
fish fingers chips and beans
was all I could afford
Formica tables florescent light

With Fred Perry shirts and Lambretta girls
Racing to the beech in the summer heat
'Pictures of Lily', 'Young Gifted and Black'
I was the most unlike lad

I used to sit and read the NME
Gambardella's on Thursday night
fish fingers chips and beans
was all I could afford
Formica tables with florescent light

Our Estate

A playful tug
that turned to fists
getting stuck
in broken lifts
That smelt of piss and cigarettes
I lived the dream with all my fiends

On our estate
We grew up fast
From Airfix kits
To burnt out cars
The girls we liked were hard to keep
Chewing gum and smoking weed

I miss my friends
Where did they go
They flew the nest
With seeds to sow
We came to blows they left like me
I guess it wasn't meant to be

Those were the treasured days
the Firework displays
That went off in my face
Maybe that's where I belonged

We pebble dashed
our council house
the neighbours weren't
in any doubt
that we'd arrived
and found our feet
my teenage years were about to seed

the ice cream van
would stop outside
and I'd be there
to wait in line
to get my tub with chocolate flake
life seemed simple on our estate

Those were the treasured days
the Firework displays
That went off in my face
Maybe that's where I belonged

On our estate
It's much improved
With Flower pots
In constant bloom
I miss the gang
Community
I guess it wasn't meant for me

What Happened

What happened to Keith
he moved to Australia
hard to believe
thought he was a failure
Must have found relief
dives in the Coral Reef
what happened to Keith

What happened to Les
died from an overdose
he was such a mess
fell asleep and slowly froze
locked inside his shed
on a makeshift bed
what happened to Les

Terry went to Prison
and served his time inside
for crimes he had committed
with a kitchen knife

What happened to John
became an architect
he could no wrong
always forging ahead

we used to share a bong
now that life has gone
what happened to John

Andy was a drummer
joined a local band
They used to play at Pontins
Down on Camber Sands

What happened to Sue
moved back to Jamaica
went back to her roots
nothing would shake her
she wore tailored suits
Doc Martin Boots
what happened to Sue

Karen joined the army
and learnt to drive a tank
once she tried to stab me
outside the old Top Rank

(What happened to me)

Guitar Avenue

I played guitar
two pieces of wood
I sat on my bed
and searched for a hook
I knew a few shapes
Some chords from a chart
I hoped that one day
I'd break a few hearts
It was all inside my head
the guitar
at the end of my bed

I play guitars
underneath the bright lights
with foot on wedge
and clouds of dry ice
I'd pull and I'd bend
All the strings on the neck
I try to look good
for all of my friends
alone with my pad and my pen
the guitar at the end of my bed

Playing a guitar
Is where I should be
Attached to my amp
The valves glow for me
with songs that ignite
a crowd in a club
it's all that I know
it's all that I love
the words that I write
lose their thread
'til I play my guitar
with my friends

Deptford

I used to live in Deptford
It was heaven for me
clinging to the rafters
while on the TV
a flat on the top floor
head in the clouds
knew all the locals
doing my rounds
Chicken Jalfrezi
round off the night
off with the fairies
holding on tight

I sat on the sofa
wrapped up in fate
the guy in the next flat
in Dire Straits
practiced all hours
I never did
he went on to big things
I slowly slipped
down snakes and ladders
But what I've got now
Is all I ever needed
With my head in the clouds

I lived for each moment
and wrote my words all day
Got drunk in the evenings
When friends came out to play

I lived by the river
with vans full of drums
amps on the back seats
smoke in my lungs
I walked with a ambition
with nowhere to go
I was in with the villains
on the front row
pubs full of bands
set up on crates
playing all of our songs
to all of our mates

I lived for each moment
and wrote my words all day
Got drunk in the evenings
When friends came out to play

I lived with a woman
Who worked for Spare Rib
She looked at my lyrics
Like I never did
She said I was sexist
I had to look it up
We listened to the Clash
And Thelonious Monk

I lived with depression
My head full of fog
the words and the music
have all long gone

I lived for each moment
and wrote my words all day
Got drunk in the evenings
When friends came out to play
and my heart to cradle the path that I took
my last days in Deptford were misunderstood

Catford

The Savoy on a Sunday
Is where we would dance
The temperature rising
As we'd try to advance
With girls on the dance floor
We'd shuffle up close
With dandruff and hackney
And socks full of holes
My head neatly shaven
I'd splash on some Brut
I was not into fighting so I started a group

We rehearsed round at Tonys
His Dad went to the pub
He said we were useless
So we played to his mum
The songs seemed to go on
For hours and days
A few chords some strumming
Mind bending displays
Of kids without focus
All stones left unturned
The escape with ambition
Was all that we learned
The Savoy on a Sunday

Was gone from my life
I was into rehearsing
We were out of our minds
I missed all the dancing
The reggae and soul
The girls were the ketchup
To my sausage roll
I dropped out completely
I threw it all away
The bus down to Catford
Stopped coming my way

The bus down to Catford
Stopped coming my way

Yellow Roses

She grew up in Peckham
In a council flat
her Mum was working evenings
her Dad was on his back
he smoked a lot of ganga
a lot of beer consumed
he woke up full of anger
and knocked Mum round the room

She grew up pretty stable
despite the atmosphere
she took up ballroom dancing
a credit for her year
she dressed in tights and sequins
she brushed her teeth at night
She fell in love with Tony
her future looking bright

She moved around the corner
worked hard to pay the rent
He taught her how to tango
She took him off to bed
they'd cuddle up together
they'd watch a small TV
she cooked him steak and Onion
they looked for harmony

CHRIS DIFFORD

She grew up round in Peckham
her journey now complete
she gave birth to her daughter
and rocked her fast asleep
she gave her all the loving
she did not receive
she takes her ballroom dancing
and sits on her knee

She grew up in Peckham
her Dad went to the rooms
he went to clear his head out
and stopped the looney tunes
he asked her for forgiveness
he watched her take the floor
she danced with yellow roses
he couldn't love her more

My Mistakes

Gilson turned up with his kit
We were all impressed by it
His playing made us all grow up
we toured local pubs
For beer and friendly hugs

Jools would ride a motorbike
in the pub he'd play all night
we'd watch him set the place alight
I'd see his left hand roll
completely in control

I found the best songs making my mistakes.

Harry scored a lot of goals
thought we were the New York Dolls
He filled a lot of empty holes
We looked on so amazed
Through flashing lights and haze

The demos always led the way
The chords we always learnt to play
The songs that made our day
With melodies and hooks
Our octaves sounded good

CHRIS DIFFORD

I found the best songs making my mistakes.

Today I make the same mistakes
Touring on the road
I was young and never thought
I'd ever be this old but that's just me
the older I get the better I used to be

Rehearsals never seem to end
The Telecaster was my friend
Playing sets then start again
I was in my teens
In T shirts and blue jeans

The Happy Eater was the place
I would fill a hungry face
Coming from a distant stage
lived of beer and fags
And sometimes cold kebabs

Today I make the same mistakes
Touring on the road
I was young and never thought
I'd ever be this old but that's just me
the older I get the better I used to be

The Last Word

She sat in her armchair
her face to the fire
his Dad was on duty
attached to a wire
that no-one could see
as he raced round the kitchen
he didn't say much
he was too busy wishing
that she would allow him
to have his opinion
she was the reason he simply didn't

he sat and watched snooker
wrapped up in the moment
while she was upstairs
in the silence she'd stolen
to read from a Bible
and pray through the window
as if god was out there
standing up on his tip toes
the balls in the pocket
had always been snookered
the secret affairs
had always been rumoured

CHRIS DIFFORD

the last word
the very last word
you know in your heart might never be heard
the last word
the very last word
she never wants to be on her own

she took to her bed
and became agoraphobic
he stayed by her side
as the cannon re loaded
each day with more powder
more verbal diarrhoea
he suffered in silence
and that's what I fear
the snapping the tutting
the eyes like a dagger
that cut you in half
but you love her and thank her

We eat cheese on toast
while we raced through each number
His father would feed us
As he'd tried to smoother
The sound of the drumming
From Mum who was sleeping
Tony would whisper
As we were all leaving
Perhaps we should practice
When she's feeling better
The band soon broke up

the last word
the very last word
you know in your heart might never be heard
the last word
the very last word
she never wants to be on her own
she never wants to be on her own

Freddie

I flew on Freddie Laker
With sandwiches to eat
Some cheese with Branston pickle
White slices with cold meat
We took off from the runway
My childhood disappeared
A chevy van was waiting
The road ahead was clear

I flew on Freddie Laker
I made my life on stage
Where I would find the answers
To scribbles on a page
Some words that might inspire
A melody and chord
And there the meak foundations
Found in polite applause

Freddie and the dreamers
Freddie and the dreamers
Freddie and the dreamers

I flew on Freddie Laker
With music on cassettes
I had a Sony Walkman
With headphones on my head
America the cherry
Upon the touring cake
The east coast and the west coast
Gave us our lucky breaks

Freddie and the dreamers
Freddie and the dreamers
Freddie and the dreamers

I stayed at The Algonquin
and walked through Central Park
I'd swagger down the sidewalk
We were on the billboard chart
I remember CBGB'S
And Freddie Laker's flight
I was dreaming of the big time
And what that might be like

Jesus

Don't be a stranger
With combed over hair
I used to see you
Out everywhere
Down to your y fronts
Up on your heels
Don't be a stranger
I know how that feels

Don't be a stranger
Angel's request
Your presence and beauty
Over the fence
By the WEM speakers
Up on the stage
Dancing like hippies
Totally cained

Don't be a stranger
Whip out your flute
Enchant with your wisdom
In your birthday suit
When I saw you leaping
I knew you'd arrived
as pigs were inflated
and made for the sky

Jesus we love you
Dancing like deer
Over the music
that I could not hear
Jesus we love you
passed on it seems
to leap through the heavens
in tide dyed blue jeans

Jesus we love you.

Plonker

my sweet piano teacher
would whisper every word
as I sat at her piano
while the pages slowly turned
my little pork chop fingers
would sometimes make her day
as I played through my homework
each note a flat away

my sweet piano teacher
was patient as a saint
my practice never perfect
each note allowed to grate
her front door neatly painted
a knocker made of brass
I sat like a good boy
but I knew it wouldn't last

pork chop fingers
pork chop fingers
who knows where they fell
a plonker on the upright
was doing very well
pork chop fingers
pork chop fingers

was all I could provide
it was not to be my forte
and the piano lessons died

My piano teacher
had not heard the Nice
the knifes were in the organ
my eyes were opened up my eyes
I missed some of my lessons
distracted by my teens
her Laura Ashley dresses
remained my distant dreams

pork chop fingers
pork chop fingers
who knows where they fell
a plonker on the upright
was doing very well
pork chop fingers
pork chop fingers
was all I could provide
it was not to be my forte
and the piano lessons died

I fell into King Crimson
And thought that Fripp was God
I loved the words the music
And became a fan of prog
I wanted to play the Organ
But not learn how to play
The piano lessons ended
There was nothing more to say

Pink Floyd

I caught the bus
And went to the gig
Sat on the grass
That's what we did
When we were young
Life was destroyed
By staying up late
Seeing Pink Floyd

I took the drugs
I could not hide
How stoned I was
Eyes open wide
Sat on my bed
My parents annoyed
That I was upstairs
Lost in Pink Floyd

I used to love
Gilmour's guitar
It shone a light
On my distant star
My head was a nest
Of songs I enjoyed
In my secret world
Caught up in Pink Floyd

Oh my oh my
Pigs might fly
I was comfortably numb
With Pink Floyd
Oh my oh my
I tripped over sky
To get to the sound
Of Pink Floyd

David and Sid
Richard and Nick
Roger who left
He was a prick
Guy took his place
We all enjoyed
Gilmour's new songs
And Pink Floyd
I sat on a ledge
12 stories high
I nearly jumped
Learning to fly
Comfortably numb
So paranoid
I would not hear
Pink Floyd

Thanks to Louise who Lino printed the sleeve for me and keeps my back at all times, I love her so much. Thank you to my manager Steve Martin, a man who is like a brother to me in many ways. And thank you to the family for bring me so much joy.

Thank you co writers and everyone who played on these records, it means the world to me.

Thank you Rachel and David at The Choir Press, without whom…

Thank you for taking time to read through my lyrics, and if you would like to hear the music that embraces these words please go to chrisdifford.com there you will find links to all of the solo albums and my gentle Podcasts which I love and record for the charity Help Musicians.

www.ingramcontent.com/pod-product-compliance
Lightning Source LLC
Chambersburg PA
CBHW031258110426
42743CB00040B/736